Communication For Change Management

Mastering Communication To Architect Change

GIFFORD THOMAS

"As leaders, communication is not a foremost thought in our heads. We assume that if we are being respectful and fair to our employees, that it is adequate. One of the most vital tools to obtaining employees' buy in, commitment and strong support is providing them with a sense of belonging via communication. Keeping them informed as they are key stakeholders within any given organization. Gifford Thomas effectively conveys this message within his book. Communicate, Communicate and Communicate.

A very thought provoking, simple and easy to read book that really brings home the point of a very basic and vital tool that is often taken for granted and overlooked by leaders. Congratulations Mr. Thomas! Looking forward to reading more of your work soon.

- Rodessia Richins, Workforce Consultant
Phd Student

"Gifford really does communicate the importance of communication for change management in this well-structured and articulate book. The subject matter is conveyed in a very engaging manner with a good balance of theory, case study examples, opinion and practical advice. Those of you familiar with change management frameworks will find this book enhances your understanding; those new to the area will find the book a useful guide."

- Mike Green, Director ~ Transitional Space
Visiting Executive Fellow ~ Henley Business School

"Communication Is The Key To Change"

CONTENTS

ACKNOWLEDGMENTS

Firstly, thanks to my beautiful wife and three children for their patience during this process. Thanks to Mike Manes, Mike Green, Mike Temple, Rodessia Richins, Abede Mack and Adelle Joseph for all your help, recommendation, encouragement and motivation. Thanks for the inspiration.

INTRODUCTION

Inspiration comes in many forms; song, poetry, movies, experiences, etc. but the underlying conduit for all inspiration is communication. Some leaders, for example, have a gift of motivating and inspiring people to believe in the impossible. When you feel inspired you become confident, you feel important, you automatically see solutions instead of problems, and that feeling somehow spreads to others.

For some, it comes natural, but for others, it is something they have to work on because they understand the power of communication and the effect it has on people. These leaders have taken companies that were close to bankruptcy and turned things around to the astonishment of many people and to the naysayers who predicted the end of the company. Four leaders immediately come to mind Steve Jobs, Howard Schultz, Anne Mulcahy and Alan Mulally. They achieved the impossible by inspiring their team to believe in their vision for the company. Let's look at these three companies a bit more in detail, and you will understand the magnitude of their problems before the transformation.

Ford

In 2007, Ford was in serious trouble and close to bankruptcy when Alan Mulally became the CEO of the company. To put Ford's position in context, listed below are some of the problems the company was facing:

- The company lost 12 billion dollars in 2006
- The demand for their vehicles declined rapidly
- Their share price was at the lowest rate ever
- The culture of the company was nauseatingly toxic
- Staff morale was the lowest it had ever been and
- There was no synergy among the various business units in the world, and the company ultimately lost its focus.

The above description looks daunting, and you may be wondering who within their right mind, would take on such a responsibility to turn around a company that lost 12 billion dollars in one year, and hemorrhaging cash at an alarming rate. Well, this was the situation at Ford in 2006, on the brink of bankruptcy and feverishly looking for someone to help turn things around.

Starbucks

In 2008, Starbucks was forced to close 600 stores in the US, their profit fell by 28 percent and in 2009, it closed another 300 stores and laid off 6,700 employees. The situation looked hopeless with a lot of people predicting that Starbucks would soon close their doors permanently in near future. However, things turned out completely different.

Apple

In 1986, this once iconic company became the laughing stock of the world. The once mighty Apple was dead in the water according to many people, with Wall Street analysts even predicting the end of

Apple to the point where Apple was practically giving away their shares.

Xerox

In 2001, Xerox had over $17 billion in debt and recorded losses in each of the preceding six years. Anne Mulcahy was named CEO of Xerox Corp to lead the turnaround, although Mulcahy was not ready for such a responsibility, she was expected to reverse the company's fortunes after a sustained period of underperformance. Four companies, four completely different industries, four different leaders, four different leadership styles, but with one commonality.

All these leaders who led these inconceivable comebacks, used communication to lead the transformation of their company. Communication was that vital link that allowed the transformation to become successful. These companies got a new awakening, and these four cases immediately come to mind.

It's interesting, I spent close to a year conducting research and investigating the communication strategies of a company involved in a transformational change, and one would think that this relatively small company, will not have the same problems as a large company like Ford or Apple, but the similarities were quite glaring.

The company had about 200 employees, and the investigation unearthed a series of problems because communication was traditionally overlooked by management as an essential vehicle to augment change and more importantly, a strategy to inspire and motivate their employees about the change. I felt the emotion when I spoke to the employees, because the word change alone, invokes a sense of fear in the hearts of many people and as a result, the lack of a coherent communication strategy made the process very confusing for many people.

The change was derailed because communication was not a prominent feature. A common theme across the literature on transformational change indicates that this type of change is hard to achieve, with more than 70% of transformational change programs failing according to John P. Kotter. Kotter made this assertion years ago, and it is still relevant today.

I am always left dumbfounded when I read this statistic given the expanse of literature available. Kotter further argued that over 100 companies try to remake themselves into significantly better competitors; a few of these corporate change efforts have been very successful, however, in most instances some have been utter failures.

Some companies have successfully implemented change throughout the length and breadth of their organization. So, this begs the question, what is the secret behind a successful transformational change, and why is it that leaders identify communication as an integral component of the change process?

This research provides valuable insight into communication and the importance of communication in a changing environment, especially if the company is undertaking a transformation change. Before I go further let's explore the situation at the company I investigated, Thomas and Co., to help you understand the context, and the approach taken by management during their change. The name of the company was changed due to a confidentiality agreement.

Thomas and Co.

In 2008, management undertook a restructuring of Thomas and Co. The CEO, as well as many managers, found it necessary to improve the company's operational efficiency, customer and stakeholder service delivery, cost effectiveness, staff commitment, and performance, to ensure the company's new objectives were achieved, and aligned to the vision for the company.

Now, this is where things got interesting. Management was plagued with many issues during the change, and the execution of such created significant problems. The culture which existed at the company was not very conducive to change, since employees already had a significant psychological attachment to their present environment. Additionally, employee's buy-in of the change was a significant problem for management, as well as, gaining support from some of the company's significant stakeholders.

Management found it extremely difficult to execute their change initiatives, and as a result, the company missed and found it extremely difficult to meet their objectives, and by extension the achievement of their new strategic direction.

After carefully analyzing their methods, I soon realized that management never took communication seriously. The leadership of the organization used a general staff meeting to inform its employees of the changes taking place at the company, but subsequent to this meeting, employees were not informed further of changes at the company and relied on "grapevine" communication for information.

Although the CEO informed line management of the importance of continuous communication with their staff, the general staff meeting was the only medium used to apprise employees of the changes occurring at the company. One can further argue, that management failed to recognize the established norms of the company and the role culture played during the change process.

Management placed more emphasis on changing the structure, systems, and processes at the company as opposed to changing their mode of communication within the organization.

What You Will Learn.

Thomas and Co. external environment was changing, and as such, the company tried to respond to this change in a quick and hastened manner. However, their lack of communication ultimately determined the outcome of their change.

This investigation was very intensive. I interviewed over 100 employees and reviewed several resources on communication in a changing environment such as scholarly articles; working papers; dissertations; research papers; professional textbooks; journals; as well as case studies. This was to ensure that all the material contained in this book was relevant and benchmarked against all the current thinking on communication in a changing environment.

You will learn:

1. Why communication is so vital during a change
2. The importance of communicating the WHY
3. Why multiple channels of communication is so important during a transformational change.
4. How your path of change determine your communication channels.
5. How to analyze your stakeholders and why you need to tailor, and segment your communication.
6. How to use communication to eradicate resistance.
7. Why the organizational and leadership culture must change to support an organization's communication efforts during the change.
8. How to eradicate grapevine type communication during the change, and the importance of formal channels of communication.
9. How to communicate with influence and a bonus chapter
10. If you want to grow as a leader, you must get comfortable with failure.

Any company regardless of its size, location, industry or sector will be involved in some form of change, it is inevitable. The world is extremely dynamic, and as the leader, you will have the responsibility to lead the change by example. As the leader, you are required to understand the crucial role communication plays during the change process because ultimately, it will determine if your change efforts are successful. Believe me, it is not rocket science, it has been done before.

When you are armed with the knowledge, understanding, and application of communication in a changing environment, you will become a dynamic, motivating and an inspirational leader who can lead any change successfully.

1 WHY COMMUNICATION IS SO VITAL DURING A CHANGE

From 1992 - 2007, Starbucks was the darling of Wall Street. The company experienced unprecedented growth, won numerous awards such as "Best Business," "Most Admired Company," "100 Best Corporate Citizens" etc. In 2007, a leaked memo from Starbucks chairman and former CEO Howard Schultz, alluded to the fracturing of Starbucks soul and boom, in the middle of the worse financial meltdown since the great depression, the company profit plummeted.

The following year, in 2008, Starbucks was forced to close 600 stores in the US, its profit fell 28 percent and in 2009, it closed another 300 stores and laid off 6,700 employees. During that time, the company's Chairman, Howard Schultz returned as CEO to lead the transformation and return the company back to its glory.

One of Schulz primary weapons used in the turnaround of Starbucks was communication. When he came back, Schultz surprised everyone when he took 10,000 store managers to New Orleans for a conference, yes, 10,000 managers in the midst of the worse time in the company history. A lot of people did not understand his decision, but Schultz knew if people were reminded of the company character and values, everyone could make a difference.

The conference was about galvanizing the entire leadership of the company—being vulnerable and transparent with their employees about how desperate the situation was, and making them understand

11

that everyone, must be personally accountable and responsible for the outcome of every single customer interaction.

Schulz used his strength as an excellent communicator to galvanize support for his turnaround. The recovery of Starbucks started with that emotional reconnection with the values of the company by the leadership. Howard Schultz inspired everyone at Starbucks to believe in the core purpose of the company again, and as a result, the company experienced a resurgence, surpassing all its company projections, and cemented their status as the leader in their industry, and one of the most recognizable brands in the world.

The lessons to be learned from the Starbucks experience is this, when you are leading a change, you must have an appreciation for communication, as a matter of fact, your plan will undoubtedly fail, if communication is not an integral aspect of your change.

According to Johnson, Scholes, and Whittington (2008), managers faced with effecting change typically underestimate substantially, the extent to which members of the organization understand the need for change, what is intended to achieve or what is involved in the change.

"The single biggest problem in communication is the illusion that it has taken place." – George Bernard Shaw

Leading change requires the use of a diverse set of communication techniques to deliver appropriate messages, assure understanding, solicit feedback, create readiness, provide a sense of urgency, and motivate recipients to act. Leaders are responsible for communicating to the organization the risks in clinging to the status quo, and the potential rewards of embracing a radically different future. Communication can be an effective tool for motivating employees involved in change, and appropriate communications provide employees with feedback and reinforcement during the change, which enables management to make better decisions and helps prepares the organization for the advantages and disadvantages to follow.

Research has proven that in the absence of a proper communication plan, the entire change process may turn into a fiasco. Emerald Research indicated that poorly managed change communication results in rumors, and resistance to change which can exaggerate the negative aspects of the change. The empirical picture that is slowly emerging indicates that communication process and organizational change implementation are inextricably linked processes.

Robertson also stated that any company's change effort is dependent on the ability of the organization to change the individual behavior of an employee. Communication with these employees should be an important, and integrative part of the change efforts and strategies. One of the primary purposes of change communication should be to inform the organizational members about the change, and how their work is altered as a result of the change.

This informative function of communication will affect your readiness for change. In Jon Wolper article, Making Change Successful, Robert Half Management Resources survey indicated that 46 percent of change management efforts, fail during execution and the reason; very often, is a lack of clear communication. "Communication is always the thing, for one reason or another, that seems to struggle through the execution stage," says Tim Hird, executive director of Robert Half Management Resources.

In the survey, 65 percent of respondents said that communicating clearly, openly and frequently, is the most critical action to take when going through organizational change. The survey also found that small companies were more susceptible to failure during the execution stage, with more than 48 percent of companies with 20-99 employees, named communication as the primary issue compared with just 29 percent of companies with more than 1,000 employees.

Good organizational communication is a crucial factor in effectively managing people, however, communication takes on a more significant role during any change process, simply because, communication reduces uncertainty, and also increases a sense of control over personal circumstances related to change and job satisfaction, according to Bordia et al. (2004).

In 2001, Anne Mulcahy was named CEO of Xerox Corp, responsible for leading a company on the edge of bankruptcy. Xerox had over $17 billion in debt and recorded losses in each of the preceding six years. Mulcahy said

"I was not ready to lead, let alone the one who was expected to reverse the company's fortunes after a sustained period of underperformance."

Wall Street also agreed, on the day Mulcahy was announced as the

CEO, Xerox stock dropped 15 percent, "a real confidence builder," she joked. But Mulcahy soon silenced her critics and led one of the greatest turnarounds in corporate history. According to Knowledge @ Wharton, under her leadership, Xerox moved from losing $273 million in 2000, to earning $91 million in 2003.

In 2004, the company's profits had reached $859 million on sales of $15.7 billion. At the same time, its stock had risen, returning 75% over the last five years, compared with a loss of 6% for the Dow Jones Total Stock Market Index. Xerox fortunes change significantly, and Mulcahy credited communication for the turnaround. According to Insights by Stanford Business, Mulcahy indicated that effective communication was perhaps the single most important component of the company's successful turnaround strategy.

"I feel like my title should be Chief Communication Officer, because that's really what I do," she said, emphasizing the importance of listening to customers and employees."

Open and honest communication with employees and customers help Mulcahy identified the problems at Xerox which was a critical component in their transformational strategies.

Communicating the Why!

In Simon Sinek's now famous Ted Talk, 'How great leaders inspire action', Sinek provided a simple but powerful model for inspirational leadership: the golden circle and the question "Why?"

According to Sinek, the fundamental difference between the "Apples" of the world and everyone else, is that they start with "why." Because Apple starts with "why" when defining their company, they are able to attract customers who share their fundamental beliefs. As Sinek puts it, "People don't buy what you do. They buy *why* you do it."

Any successful change begins with the answer to one of the most fundamental questions about change: Why? It is human nature to want to understand the reasoning behind an action or a required change. Management should clearly explain the business drivers or opportunities that have resulted in the need for change.

It also means addressing why a change is needed now, and explaining the risk of not changing. Schultz achieved this in New Orleans when he clearly communicated to all the 10,000 managers, the risk of clinging to the status quo, notwithstanding the fact that the conference cost the company about 30 million dollars, this solidified how important the conference was to Howard Schultz.

Communication in a changing environment is one of the most critical variables one has to consider when initiating a change. According to Hiatt (2006), employees want to hear why the change is occurring, and how the change aligns with the vision of the organization from the business leaders. Explaining the why is absolutely important even if it cost 30 million dollars.

Appropriate communication will significantly help employees understand the reasons for the change as well as, the effects of the change. According to the researchers, this is the first requirement if the transformation has any chance of success. Many experts indicated that communication is indispensable when persuading people to support change. Some researchers have even claimed that the essence of change is communication. The first questions people want answered are:

- Why are we making this change?
- Why now?
- How will this change improve things?
- What's wrong with the status quo?
- How will this change affect me?

One of the main components of a successful communication strategy, is the selection of appropriate communication channels. In the next chapter, we will explore the various communication channels, and how the change complexity or the lack thereof, will determine what channels are best suited for the success of the change.

2 COMMUNICATION CHANNELS

"It is not what you say, is how you say it"

Employees need to have an overall picture of what the organization is trying to achieve, the question we will be answering now is, 'what communication channel is best suited to explain the why, and how to keep staff informed about the change to allay their fears and concerns as well to keep your team inspire and motivated throughout the process.

When Steve Jobs return as the CEO of Apple in 1987, Jobs was presenting the 'Think Different' campaign for the first time to Apple staff. Do you remember the Think Different ad,

"this is for the crazy ones, the misfits, the square pegs in a round hole",

Think Different was the mantra used by Jobs to turnaround Apple. Just imagine in 1986, there was a web campaign to get Apple fans to buy a few shares of the company to show Wall Street that Apple was still relevant, believe or not. When Steve Jobs returned, the fortune of Apple changed significantly, and that's putting it very mildly.

Ryan Faas wrote in his article "If you had told me when I was reporting on Apple's change in leadership, that the company would eventually have a market cap that topped Exxon Mobil's -- making it the most valuable company in the U.S. (and exceeding Microsoft and Intel combined) -- or that it would have more cash on hand than the United

States itself, I'd have called you crazy. And yet that happened under Jobs' leadership".

Wall Street analyst predicted Apple demise, and even suggested that the company should give away their share because no one will buy them. Well, Jobs had a different Idea; with courage and determination, Apple returned to profitability, and became the most valuable company in the world.

But the turnaround of Apple started with:

1. The return of Jobs and
2. The meeting with Apple staff when Jobs launched the "Think Different" campaign.

Jobs spoke with emotion, sincerity, and explained at length why Apple became one of the most valuable brands in the world. He started with the WHY and also explained the benefits and consequence if the company did not change. Harvard university professor John P. Kotter, indicated that poor communication in many instances is the root cause of many failed change efforts in many organization, and without a lot of credible communication, employee's hearts and minds are never captured. As a result, organizations who continually adopt this practice will continue to experience problems during any change process.

When trying to achieve any change, your communication channels are critical. It can literally make or break your process as a result, significant thought should go into its execution, especially during your planning and streamlining of the change. Let's explore the various communication channels, and how the nature of the change will determine what communication channel is most appropriate.

Types of Communication Channels

Face to face Communication

- team briefing
- conferences
- presentations and speeches
- one to one meeting

Audio Conferencing

- Video Conferencing
- Video/DVD
- Business TV

Print-Based

- Circulars and Memos
- Magazines and Newsletter
- Manuals and Handbook
- Brochures and Report

Computer Based communication

- emails
- intranet
- corporate portals

Social Media

- Enterprise Social Networks

- Blogs
- Wikis
- Slack
- Spark
- Flipgrid
- Slack
- WhatApp
- Instagram
- YouTube
- Linkedin

The investigation into Thomas and Co. unveiled some very startling management practices during the change. One of the more glaring occurrences was the passiveness in which management communicated with their staff. But what was even more astounding, is the fact that management did not employ multiple channels of communication to disseminate information to staff about the change, but continued to use a general staff meeting as the main channel of communication to outline the change process.

From the interviews conducted at Thomas and Co, all the interviewees agreed that the use of this general staff meeting to outline the upcoming changes was not ideal, since the forum was quite inadequate for disseminating any real information about the change. Incorporating a variety of communication channels during the change, will ensure that the message from management is received by every employee in the organization, since all individuals will react to change differently and in the process, contribute to the change base on their degree of information received.

A number of communication strategies according to Balogun and Hope Hailey (1999), are designed to employ different communicating medium, since participants will never remember everything from one communication channel during a transformational change. Thus, other mediums can provide useful backup such as using reference material for a different group of employees to give further understanding to employees who are confused about the change.

Some staff required a richer form of communication (we will address this later), and the responsibility lies with the leadership of the organization, to simplify the message and tailor what is communicated to staff. Effective communication channels are that vital tool one can use to reinforce senior management commitment to employees during the change process, and to alleviate any confusion in the minds of employees about a pending or ongoing change.

Your change complexity will determine what channels of communication is suitable or required. Additionally, to build that awareness in the company, the right communication channels must be used. One of the early indicators that a problem existed at Thomas and Co was the lack of awareness of the change, and the lack of excitement among staff. Some staff was not aware of the change, and as a result, an effective communication channel is that critical component one has to employ, to create that awareness among all employees to ensure the change is successful.

Choosing The Right Channel/s

Fig 1

Effective and Ineffective Communication of Change

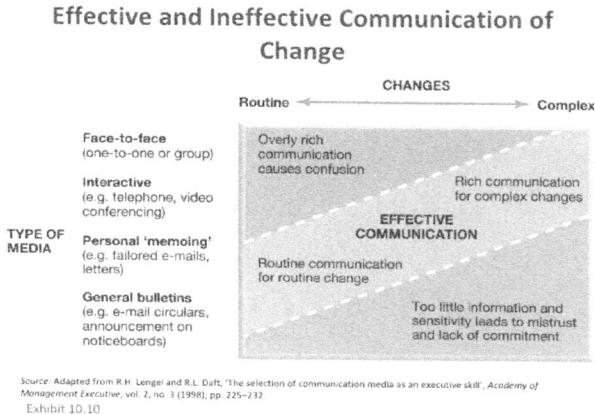

CHANGES

Routine ←————————————————→ Complex

TYPE OF MEDIA

Face-to-face (one-to-one or group)

Interactive (e.g. telephone, video conferencing)

Personal 'memoing' (e.g. tailored e-mails, letters)

General bulletins (e.g. e-mail circulars, announcement on noticeboards)

Overly rich communication causes confusion

Rich communication for complex changes

EFFECTIVE COMMUNICATION

Routine communication for routine change

Too little information and sensitivity leads to mistrust and lack of commitment

Source: Adapted from R.H. Lengel and R.L. Daft, 'The selection of communication media as an executive skill', *Academy of Management Executive*, vol. 2, no. 3 (1998), pp. 225–232.

Exhibit 10.10

When planning your change, the key to choosing a communication channel according to Balogun and Hope Hailey (1999), is to match it to the audience needs. Non-routine, complex change requires a richer form of message and meaning, and as such, face to face and interactive channels as mentioned in fig 1 above, has a more significant impact than any other single medium. These rich channels allow for:

- Rapid feedback.

- A high level of intimacy between employees and management

- Quick adaptation to employee concerns, in which management can directly respond to signals (mimic and gesture) from employees.

Face to face communication allows participants to pick up non-verbal cues as the interaction unfolds, adds richness to the message, as well as communicate emotional aspects of the communication which otherwise, might be hidden.

Remember how Steve Jobs communicated with emotion when he spoke to his employees about the "Think Different" campaign. That emotional aspect of the communication is vital, because it allowed his team to see and most importantly feel his emotion. That richest in the message was transparent, and felt by everyone in that room and anyone watching via video etc.

Face to face communication also clarifies ambiguities, and according to O'Connor (1990), provides the opportunity for immediate feedback to correct deficiencies which may occur in the communication process.

Fig 2 Paths of Change

| | Extent of change | |
	Transformation	Realignment
Incremental	**Evolution:** Transformational change implemented gradually through inter-related initiatives; likely to be proactive change undertaken in participation of the need for future change	**Adaptation:** Change undertaken to realign the way in which the organisation operates; implemented in a series of steps
Big Bang	**Revolution:** Transformational change that occurs via simultaneous initiatives on many fronts: • more likely to be forced and reactive because of the changing competitive conditions that the organisation is facing	**Reconstruction:** Change undertaken to realign the way in which the organisation operates with many initiatives implemented simultaneously: • often forced and reactive because of a changing competitive context

(Speed of change — Incremental / Big Bang)

Regardless of your company's path of change during its

24

transformational journey as mentioned above in fig 2, face to face communication should be your primary option with useful backup from other channels. One of the major problems at Thomas and Co., was management continued reliance on this general staff meeting to make staff aware of the changes at the company. Remember the changes at Thomas and Co. was transformational:

- The organization structure was changed

- Employees were deployed in new positions

- The strategic focus of the company was changed

If you are leading in that type of environment or if you are making significant changes, your communication cannot be routine. According to Johnson, Scholes, and Whittington (2005), to communicate a highly complex set of changes, it would be inappropriate to use standardized bulletins and circulars. Management, however at Thomas and Co. persisted with this one routine channel of communication. Although employees had a lot of concerns about the changes, and there was no personal follow up meeting between employees and management to allay their fears.

The research is clear, one routine channel of communication to outline a complex change is inadequate; there must be follow-up and avenues for staff to give, and solicit feedback about the change from management, particularly if the changes to be introduced are challenging.

It is absolutely necessary to decide which channel is best suited to the audience and the message being delivered. You need to match the communication channel strategy to the context of the design choices. For example, if the change style is communication and education, then there may be need to have seminars or training education to make staff aware of the changes.

Fig 3 - Change kaleidoscope

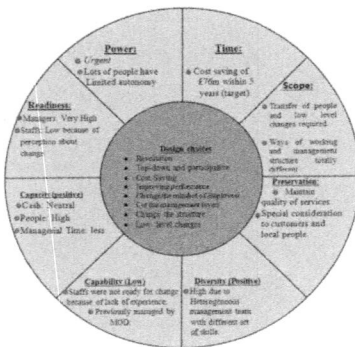

Design choices

Design choices represent the key features of a change management approach:

- **Change path** - clarifying the types of change in terms of timescales, the extent of change and the desired outcomes.
- **Change start point** - where the change is initiated (e.g. top-down or bottom up).
- **Change style** - which management style should be adopted (e.g. collaborative, participative, directive or coercive)?

- **Change interventions** - which mechanisms should be deployed (e.g. education, communication, cultural interventions)?
  - **Change roles** - assigning roles and responsibilities (e.g. leadership, use of consultants, role of change action teams).

Source: Kaplan Financial Knowledge Bank

For example, if the change style is communication and education, then there may be need to have seminars or training education to make staff aware of the changes. It is important to note that adopting face to face as the only mode of communication can be very detrimental to the whole process as well. Face-to-face communication does not obviate the need for other communication efforts. Although, this form of communication channel clearly has its advantages, solely adopting this medium, can prove to be very harmful during a complex or transformational change.

Moreover and this is very important; adopting a rich form of communication like face to face meeting for routine change, will **confuse** the hell out of your employees and waste a lot of time. On the flip side, if you adopting a routine form of communication during a complex change, **it will lead to mistrust** and a **lack of awareness** about the change and this occurred at Thomas and Co.

Removing a damaged chair and replacing it with a new one does not require a face-to-face meeting, that's wasting time and energy. That information can simply be conveyed by an email. However, changing the strategic focus, culture etc., of a company will require a face-to-face meeting, as well other forms of communication to provide clarity and more details.

Social Media

Social media can be a valuable "vehicle" to promote better and faster change management because we spend nearly three hours per day on social platforms. More than half of employers are already using internal social media and as such, many companies have an opportunity to leverage social media as a significant change management tool.

According to a recent study by Weber Shandwick conducted in partnership with KRC Research; 55% of respondents who had gone through a change event at work said they wished their employer offered more digital and social engagement, while 42% said they wanted more face-to-face communication.

Whether companies are using enterprise social networks like blogs, wikis, or platforms like Slack, Spark, and Flipgrid, companies can leverage these social media platforms to help manage the change at their organization. Internal social media can help flatten the organization and drive transparent dialogue across levels, functions, and geographies.

When longtime Cisco CEO, John Chambers stepped down to serve as chairman in July 2015, and was replaced by Chuck Robbins, the company started two simultaneous Jive threads—one inviting employees to thank John, and another asking: "What advice or suggestions do you have for Chuck Robbins as he transitions to CEO?" Within four days the two posts drew over 1,000 comments, and over 20,000 views. Similar employee crowdsourcing efforts have been used to redefine company values (at IBM), and generate ideas for cutting operational costs (at BASF). It may no longer be an option for management to ignore Social Media when managing change; the potential benefits are too substantial to ignore!

There is also no need to get overly technical. By leveraging your existing platforms and getting creative with platforms like Slack, WhatsApp, Instagram, YouTube, or whatever is appropriate to your organization and the particular change project, you can breathe new life into the way you manage change.

It's important to note that social media alone won't lead to higher employee engagement during change. Face-to-face communication, manager's support, and real-time coaching, are all critical to preserving trust and boosting morale and performance in times of change. But social media is fast becoming an indispensable supplement. Research has shown that 88% of employees use at least one social media at home, and that many want a similar experience at work.

It's clear that social is becoming a critical component of any change plan. Consider Zappos' CEO Tony Hsieh, who announced layoffs for 8% of the company's workforce on Zappos' external blog immediately after sending an internal email. Employees appreciated the transparency, and later engaged with Tony, each other, and Zappos' stakeholders over Twitter. The open conversation provided Zappos with insight into how best to handle sensitive situations, fostered thoughtful, public interaction between management and employees, and even helped some laid-off workers find future employment with other companies.

Social media cannot be ignored but as the leader, you must ensure that you don't let employees post harmful and hurtful messages about others according to Dr. Carol A. Beatty. Many organizations have found that employee productivity can go down when they spend too much time on social media.

Communication success will occur when rich media is used for non-routine change, and routine communication is used for routine change. One must agree that general communication is critical towards a successful change process; the richness of face-to-face communication is undeniable; however, it is absolutely necessary to decide which channel is best suited to the audience and the message being delivered.

CASE STUDY 1 - THE TRANSFORMATIONAL CHANGE AT HONG KONG and SHANGHAI BANKING CORPORATION (HSBC)

HSBC is the second largest financial institution in the world with a long established history in banking. The bank has approximately 10,000 offices in seventy-seven countries, and is considered one of the major players in the world of banking.

However, in the late 1990's management recognized that the banking environment was changing, and to ensure that the bank remained in the league of top ten banks in the world by market capitalization. HSBC introduced a bank-wide strategic culture change programme called 'Together, We Win' (TWW!). As an integral aspect of their change strategies, communication took on a prominent role during the process.

Phase 1 of the change process involved over 15,000 staff from HSBC Holdings Hong Kong, plus five subsidiary companies. They attended a one-day event between November 2000, and July 2001. At this event, the facilitators and top management cemented the reasoning for the change. Reinforcing the core values in their presentation and answering questions from staff.

Phase two involved transferring the learning event to the multi-faceted local workplace of over 15,000 staff by providing customized learning tools to help the staff embrace the change in their local workplace. The programme was implemented in the workplace during normal work duties. Teams would apply the programme's core values with support and reinforcement from their team leaders and identified line champions. A TWW! booklet was produced and circulated to every staff member. The booklet explained the linkage between the TWW! core values and HSBC group's strategic imperatives, and also articulated to staff how each individual could contribute to the group strategy in their own roles.

After 2.5 years of changing their culture, HSBC achieved significant benefits and the outcome yielded an ROI of 606.3%. But what is important to note is that the bank recognized the need to build a culture of trust during the process, and did not fall victim to a quick fix or implementing the change from a top down approach.

The leadership in their wisdom used the one day event to explain the reasoning for the change (face to face), took questions from employees, and supplemented their one day event with other forms of communication channels such as booklets. Management utilized the appropriate communication channels to facilitate their change and as result, their change initiatives was a success.

Questions

1. What were the channels of communication use by management?

2. Do you think the channels were suitable for the change?

3. Can you identify where in the case management communicated the WHY

3 TAILORING YOUR COMMUNICATION AND MAINTAINING CONSISTENCY IN YOUR MESSAGE

Stakeholders Analysis

According to Dr. Carol A. Beatty, effective communications depend partly on knowing who the stakeholders are, and how they should be included in communications initiatives. Most of the research shows that organizations should err on the side of more involvement and two-way communications rather than less. To make these critical decisions, Dr. Beatty recommended a structured approach that involves several steps:

1. Identifying the stakeholders with whom you need to communicate about the change

2. Mapping the degree of influence and impact for each stakeholder

3. Defining what their interests in the change initiative are likely to be

4. Deciding on the communication and involvement approach, you will take with each stakeholder

Identifying Your Stakeholders

Dr. Beatty also indicated that the leader should decide who the main stakeholders in this change will be. Who will be most and least impacted by it, for example:

- Senior leadership groups
- Certain senior executives
- Management groups
- Certain managers
- Supervisors
- Specific departments or divisions
- Employees
- Union(s) or union officers
- Clients

Stakeholder Map

The second task according to Dr. Carol A. Beatty is to segment these stakeholders into groups by degree of influence, and degree of impact. This will help you tailor your communications and involvement approaches to each group.

Fig 4 - Stakeholder Map

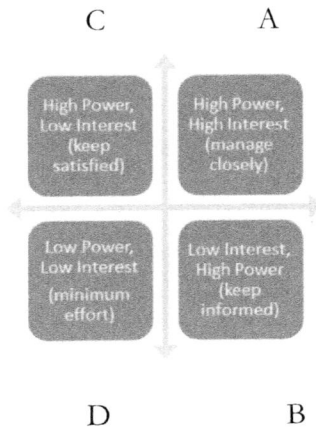

C   A

High Power, Low Interest (keep satisfied)

High Power, High Interest (manage closely)

Low Power, Low Interest (minimum effort)

Low Interest, High Power (keep informed)

D   B

Source: 5th Edition PMBOK® Guide—Chapter 13: Analyzing Stakeholder Engagement

One suitable method to classify your stakeholders according to Dr. Carol A. Beatty is to write the name of each stakeholder on a Post-it note, and then to discuss where to put that stakeholder on the map.

That way you can move the Post-it notes around before you decide on a final placement. The first decision criterion for placement is the degree of impact. In other words, how much will the proposed change impact each stakeholder's daily work life?

A lot? A little?

Then discuss the degree of influence. How much influence should you allow each stakeholder to have over this change? A lot? A little? How much should they contribute? Should they have a veto over certain decisions? After grouping the stakeholders, you can more easily decide on a communication approach for each.

Quadrant A

Stakeholders in quadrant A, those who will be highly impacted by the change, and who will exercise a lot of influence over the project, will have important roles as decision makers, planners, and doers. You'll get the best results by working closely with these stakeholders, so a high level of communication and involvement is required for them.

Quadrant B

Stakeholders in quadrant B will have to adapt to the change, but will have minimal influence on decisions about planning and implementation. Employee groups are often found here. The stakeholder map recommends that you inform and instruct groups in quadrant B about the change. You tell them what's happening and explain in detail how the move is going to affect them.

The objective is to develop their understanding of the change, but it's always wise to go beyond merely informing and instructing if you can. The research is clear: If you want cooperation, then consulting the employees about their needs and interests will definitely help.

Solicit their feedback on essential aspects of the change that will be relevant to them. Furthermore, you may want to involve them in some aspects of the change. Of course, this has to be done within parameters set by the steering committee or project team.

Quadrant C

Who do you think will exercise a high degree of influence over the change project but will not be as highly impacted by it as those in quadrant A? These stakeholders will be in quadrant C. I often find senior management in this quadrant if the change is not a large strategic initiative. Seek help from stakeholders in quadrant C by informing, involving and consulting them at crucial times and by getting their commitment to action. They can also be influential experts and role models. Enlist their help. These employees will be excellent change agents for the company.

Quadrant D

Quadrant D stakeholders will not be highly impacted by the change and will have a low degree of impact on the design of the change project. These stakeholders will have the least communication needs, but your objective should be to make them aware of the change. Your approach will be to merely inform them about the change initiative and what you are trying to achieve with it.

But what level of participation is optimal and in what types of change decisions? Abraham Sagie and Meni Koslowski found that subordinate involvement in tactical decisions, as opposed to strategic decisions, was a better predictor of an increase in change acceptance.

The third task in stakeholder analysis is to find out what each stakeholder's issues are likely to be, which will help you address their concerns in your communications to them. Do not guess what their issues are. Online, telephone, and mail surveys are the most efficient method to uncover them, especially when there are a lot of stakeholders to contact.

Focus groups of representative groups of stakeholders can be used to drill down and also to create content for survey questions. Interviews are effective but time-consuming and best used to discover as much information as possible, from highly influential stakeholders. Remember: this is an iterative process, not a one-time action, and it is very important. One respected researcher found that fully half of the decisions studied failed, because the decision makers did not consider the interests and information held by stakeholders sufficiently.

The fourth and final task is to design communications that addresses each stakeholder's issues. One size does not fit all. For example, during a reorganization initiative, some departments may be affected more than others. The highly affected groups will need much more information and details about how their jobs will change, if group membership will change, if they will be relocated and if so, where, etc. Departments that will be less affected will not be interested in this level of detail.

Each stakeholder group is unique, so communications should be tailored to each group's specific interests, even though the message must remain consistent across groups.

Endlessly repeating the message and maintaining consistency in your message

After identifying your stakeholders and communicating the change via many communication channels, it is vital to endlessly repeat the message of the change and never believe that your staff has heard it too many times, especially during a transformational or complex change.

One cannot assume that communicating the change once or twice via many communication channels is sufficient. Even if staff understood the change or have a deep-seated understanding of the change process, continuous repetition of the change is extremely important to get buying from staff, as well as keeping staff continuously informed. According to Prosci, it is important to repeat key messages a number of times. The first time you announce a change to employees, they are often wondering how it will impact them. You want to ensure your key messages make an imprint in your employee's subconscious mind, share the messages more often than you think you need to.

For example, have you ever done anything throughout your day on complete auto-pilot? Simple tasks that you get done without thinking about, your subconscious mind is responsible for that automatic behavior like your habits, and it takes over routine tasks and helps you to do them automatically.

Picture it like this; your subconscious mind is like a huge memory bank. Its capacity is virtually unlimited, and it permanently stores everything that ever happens to you. By the time you reach the age of 21, you have already permanently stored more than one hundred times the contents of the entire Encyclopedia Britannica.

It has memorized all your comfort zones, and it works to keep you in them. Every time you try to create a new habit, your subconscious is pulling you right back to what is familiar. Try this experiment, hold your palm up in front of your face and imagine that you have a lemon on your right palm before your eyes.

Do you experience your mouth watering? The conscious mind knows that there is no lemon and it's only your imagination. The subconscious mind is illogical, and immediately believes the imaginary data put in your mind, and as a result your mouth waters.

Put simply, what you focus on, you attract. Any thought that is repeated over and over again will take an imprint within the subconscious mind. It's the same with your communication. Your message will eventually take an imprint in your employee's subconscious mind when it is repeated over and over again. New behaviors will start to manifest itself at your company to the point where it becomes a habit.

Additionally, the consistency of that message is vitally important. In Dr. Lily Cheng's research on the 9 Enablers of Change, Consistency of Change Message was identified as one of the main enablers to change. According to the research, maintaining the consistency of the message ensures alignment across the change team, making sure that only "one voice" or "same language" is being spoken. The consistency in the message would also help implement change successfully, by reducing ambiguity and confusion.

Management needs to hold regular sessions with their staff, to allay their fears of the change and continuously explain how the staff fits into the overall strategic plan of the organization, while maintaining consistency in their message. At Thomas and Co., the information from the general staff meeting was totally contradictory from what the department managers was communicating to their team. This added to the confusion and that inconsistency led to a highenten level of resistance of the change.

When Alan Mulally arrived at Ford as the CEO, one of his priorities was identifying Ford's core purpose and charting a vision for Ford recovery. Mulally found an ad from 1925 in which Henry Ford outlined his purpose for the company:

"Opening the highways for all mankind."

Mulally had that ad blown up and mounted on his wall. He passed out copies to each of Ford's top executives.

Mulally made sure that all future product decisions would be weighed against that promise. The core purpose was used as the guiding light for the company and reignited the fire that somehow got extinguished. Ford required a change of focus, vision, strategy, and culture. The glue that held all the components together inside and outside of the company was communication.

Fig 5 - One Ford Plan

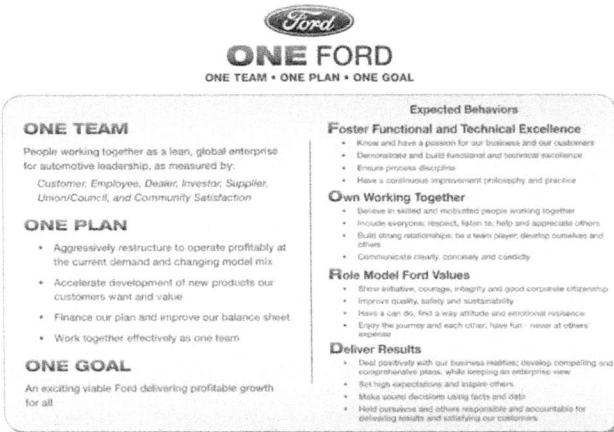

ONE FORD
ONE TEAM • ONE PLAN • ONE GOAL

ONE TEAM

People working together as a lean, global enterprise for automotive leadership, as measured by:

Customer, Employee, Dealer, Investor, Supplier, Union/Council, and Community Satisfaction

ONE PLAN

- Aggressively restructure to operate profitably at the current demand and changing model mix
- Accelerate development of new products our customers want and value
- Finance our plan and improve our balance sheet
- Work together effectively as one team

ONE GOAL

An exciting viable Ford delivering profitable growth for all

Expected Behaviors

Foster Functional and Technical Excellence
- Know and have a passion for our business and our customers
- Demonstrate and build functional and technical excellence
- Ensure process discipline
- Have a continuous improvement philosophy and practice

Own Working Together
- Believe in skilled and motivated people working together
- Include everyone; respect, listen to, help and appreciate others
- Build strong relationships; be a team player; develop ourselves and others
- Communicate clearly, concisely and candidly

Role Model Ford Values
- Show initiative, courage, integrity and good corporate citizenship
- Improve quality, safety and sustainability
- Have a can do, find a way attitude and emotional resilience
- Enjoy the journey and each other; have fun - never at others' expense

Deliver Results
- Deal positively with our business realities; develop compelling and comprehensive plans, while keeping an enterprise view
- Set high expectations and inspire others
- Make sound decisions using facts and data
- Hold ourselves and others responsible and accountable for delivering results and satisfying our customers

Source: Ford Annual Report 2015

The team developed their One Ford Plan, which became the reference point for the transformation. Mulally had this plan printed on wallet cards and distributed to every Ford employee. He opened every weekly meeting by reviewing them. He recited them in every speech, in every town hall meeting, in every press conference.

One of the most critical variable used to achieve the transformation was a compelling vision, clarity of strategy, open and honest communication, and a change of values. Mulally ensured that his communication was constant and consistent to point where people got fed up of hearing the four-point plan.

Mulally went at lengths to communicate and make people feel comfortable about the change, and to explain their role in the process.

43

One of the most notable illustrations of this point may relate to the fact that Mulally had managed to move his office from top floor to the fourth floor, where engineers were based so he can be available for communication and to provide a more 'hands-on' approach.

During the change implementation period, there were frequent occasions when Mulally would respond to emails from employees by attending their offices in person, or calling them to discuss relevant issues (Hoffman, 2012).

His positive influence over the company eventually caught on, when you have open and honest communication in your business, it will remove any ambiguity and allow your employees to trust the plan, trust the process, and most importantly trust the leader.

Effective communication means identifying your stakeholders, tailoring your communication, endlessly repeating the message, and having consistency with the message with all stakeholders.

4 TOP LEADERSHIP COMMITMENT AND A LINE MANAGER'S ROLE

The research is absolutely clear; line managers are a crucial relevance bridge between top management and lower level members of the organization. Why! Because they are in touch with the day to day routines of the organization which can so quickly become blockages to change, and the climate for change that can help or hinder change. They are in a position to translate change initiatives into a locally, relevant form of message, according to Johnson, Scholes, and Whittington (2005).

Line managers' one to one communication with staff during a significant change is vitally important. With the absence of this form of communication from their line manager, employees can be become extremely confused. One has to understand, that change engenders fear regardless of the circumstance, and some people are very wary of change. Without that communication from their line manager, an employee's resistance to the change is very high. Managers therefore, can contribute significantly to galvanizing commitment, or add to the resistance and cause a blockage of the change.

When a change is ongoing, a manager or supervisor is in the best position to help employees understand the reason for the change according to Hiatt (2006). Additionally, managers should discuss change with their employees through face to face communication, employing one-on-one sessions and group meetings.

It is worth mentioning again, an employee's manager will help reinforce the change immensely using an active communication channel, especially in the initial stages of a transformational change. One to one communication has always proven to be very appropriate, since managers can help ease the confusion which may occur, but more importantly, provide that degree of certainty that the change will benefit the organization strategically.

During a change, your line managers must be that principal change agent. What is a change agent? A change agent is an individual or group, that helps effect change in an organization, and as a result, the change agent is seen as the one or group that motivates, inspire, and lead the change by example, with the intention to influence a positive outlook of the change.

If however, staff recognizes that their manager or the leadership has no apparent interest in the change, it will automatically filter down to the team that the change is not that important. This was quite apparent at Thomas and Co. The fact that the general staff meeting was the only channel of communication used during the change, and managers were unaware of the details of the change, indicated to staff that this change was not important.

It is worth mentioning that the culture of the organization, but more specifically the leadership culture, facilitated this lack of communication, and this contributed significantly towards the communication crisis that occurred at Thomas and Co.

Leadership Culture

The culture of a company is directly influenced by the leader, feeding off the urgency of the management team. If management wants to create an entirely new approach to communicating with staff, a culture change should be a priority. Well established routines can be a severe blockage to change.

When Mulally arrived at Ford, one of his first acts as CEO, was to shatter the traditional management culture that existed at Ford. Mulally invested significantly in formulating a clear vision for the Ford brand, soliciting the company stakeholders in general, and members of the workforce in particular to share the one Ford vision. His effective communication with the employees, and a high level of personal engagement in dealing with change can be specified as another essential aspect of Mulally's change management style. Mulally was always equipped with his optimism and smile throughout the difficult period at Ford; this proved to be very instrumental in terms of improving employee morale and productivity.

Moreover, Mulally has efficiently served as the principal change agent for Ford Motor Company, by communicating the reasons and benefits of each change proposal to company stakeholders. Selling all company corporate jets but one, and minimizing other perks for top executives including himself during cost-saving initiatives (Gallo, 2012). This illustrated Mulally's strong commitment to the changes that were being implemented.

Importantly, change proposals drafted and implemented by Mulally met minimum resistance from employees at all levels (Herbold, 2011), even though sizable members of the workforce were significantly disadvantaged because of these changes. This achievement can be explained through the display of charisma, outstanding leadership skills, and the understanding by Mulally that effective communication is a necessity if the changes being proposed, and implemented are successful.

According to Schein (1992), organizational culture is a direct result of a leader's behavior and values, but more importantly, leadership values are crucial to understanding corporate behavior, since people tend to emulate the behavior of their leaders with the assumption that their behavior is right.

Role modeling is an effective strategy to facilitate change; however, leaders must be prepared to walk the talk of change, as illustrated in Fig 6, to instill any credibility during the change process. It is important to note that a leadership culture that is ill-defined can create unclear cues for what is important (purpose and task focus), and how employees should act, as it relates to the organization culture.

If the CEO and the management team expect employees to buy into the change, they must be the role models for that change. They must lead by example, and create a culture that allows employees to accept the changes at the organization. Peus at el. (2009), indicated that managers are a filter of information regarding imminent change, but more importantly, the communication of this information should be relevant and understandable to their employees.

Allen et al. (2007), recommended the use of a cascading approach to developing change communication with line managers conveying more practical information to their employees.

It is interesting to note, according to Fig 4 above, that communication during a change requires a different strategy at different stages during the process. One can clearly deduce that a CEO's role, and a line manager's role during the unfreeze, move, and sustain process, is critical to ensure that employees understand their roles since insufficient follow-up, and a lack of fine-tuning once implementation begins, can lead to resistance from staff.

One can observe the direct correlation between the lack of communication, and the significant heighten level of resistance during the change. After the general staff meeting at Thomas and Co., communication was limited, and as a result, this brewed an increased level of resistance from employees during the change. Management at Thomas and Co. were the guardians of the status quo; although top management indicated the need for more communication, none was forthcoming. The longer management waited to communicate the details of their change process according to Hiatt (2006), the longer staff takes to make the necessary adjustment to their psychological contract, and as a direct consequence, this derailed the whole change initiatives.

Thomas and Co's. organizational culture were highly susceptible to the influence of leadership behavior, and the fact that the department managers were lacking important details about the change created a very toxic culture, with many employees quite confused as to the need for this radical change.

Transformational leadership was needed, but this was sorely missing. Managers who were supposed to be the principal agent of change, showed no urgency to change their mode of communication, but more importantly, showed no necessity to communicate the change to their respective staff and as a result, this led to resistance by many employees.

Change must be anchored firmly in the organizational culture to last, and continuously work throughout the transformational journey to attain any success. However, to accomplish this, communication must be central to an organization's success. Line managers in many instances, are more appropriate to translate change, but top leadership should set the example. The role of the line manager becomes extremely important where this is concern.

During my investigation, that supervisor-subordinate, two-way communicative processes was missing. Some line managers were very skeptical of the changes taking place and as a result, the management team was not unified in their position about the change, and this also created a lot of problems. If the line managers, who are responsible for disseminating information about the change and is considered the principle change agents in within their department, does not buy into the change, there will be a communication breakdown in the respective unit and by extension the company.

The departmental manager's role in the change solicited some fascinating comments from the interviewees. For example, one interviewee indicated that:

"Managers were not aware of the details of the change."

When asked further about the interviewee's experience in any meeting with their manager, it was quite surprising to learn that the information was not consistent with the information coming from the general staff meeting.

It's important to note that line managers are more appropriate to translate change into language and terminology that is relevant to their staff but if these managers are limited in their knowledge of the change or don't agree with the change or have concerns about the change, it will create a culture of mistrust and confusion.

In the initial stages of a transformational change, it is important that managers provide that rich form of communication since this is critical to the whole change process. But for some strange reason, this was never done by the various departmental managers at Thomas and Co., and as a result, this heightens the level of resistance throughout the process. As the manager, you have to be on point with your message, especially during a change, any element of inconsistency will spark rumors and confusion in the minds of your employees. Management failed to recognize the established norms at the agency, and the role culture played during the change process. Management placed more emphasis on changing the structure, systems, and processes at the company, as opposed to the cultural element in the organization.

The introduction of structural changes only scratches the surface of any transformation effort according to Kets de Vries*, Guillén Ramo, and Korotov of INSEAD (2009). The fact that a significant amount of behavior takes place at an unconscious level, mindset changes are not easily accomplished. As a result, the strategic objectives of the organization are not achieved as illustrated in fig 9 above.

The CEO has to empower the line managers and hold them accountable for their actions, especially the communication with staff. A communication audit should be initiated, to ensure that the correct information is disseminated to staff. Managers need to be more involved in the change with some degree of accountability, however; this can only happen if there is some form of culture change and cohesion at the leadership level of the organization.

A good friend, Mike Manes from Square One Consulting use this presentation to show leaders that a cohesive management team is necessary to achieve successful change. In the presentation, Mike held a dollar bill in one hand and 100 pennies in the other. Mike explained that each hand holds a dollar – they have equal value.

They can buy the same things, however if you toss the dollar bill in the air and let it float to the ground the dollar is easy to pick up – it is a single unit. If you throw the pennies in the air – you get CHAOS. Leaders too often begin transformational change before they create a cohesive unit with a shared PURPOSE, VISION, VALUES, AND MISSION.

5 FORMAL OR INFORMAL COMMUNICATION

Before Howard Schultz announced to the world that he was returning as the CEO of Starbucks, Schultz told one person, his friend Michael Dell. While on a bike ride, Dell indicated to Schultz that he should develop a transformative agenda outlining the change from start to finish and communicating that plan to all the employees at Starbucks. It was a similar situation with Dell a year before when he returned as the CEO of the company he founded.

On January 6th, 2008, Howard Schultz wrote a letter to all the partners at Starbucks announcing his return as the CEO of Starbucks. In the letter, Schultz outlined the purpose of the change, the objectives, and the series of activities that led to the fracturing of the Starbucks sprit.

Schultz indicated and I quote:

"Twenty-five years ago, I walked into Starbucks first store in Seattle's Pike Place Market, and from that day forward we have taken the road less traveled. Working with an exceptional group of people and summoning all the courage we could muster, we created a new kind of place ? one that served the kind of coffee that most people had never tasted, an environment that didn't look like any other store, and hiring people who were fanatically passionate about coffee and celebrated their interaction with customers. To do this, we focused every ounce of our beings on creativity and innovation.

Over the years, together we have built one of the most recognized and respected brands in the world. When we went public in June 1992, we had 119 stores. We now have more than 15,000 stores and a significant and growing presence in 43 countries, serving 50 million customers a week. These customers have placed their trust in us, and for them and for each other we need to ensure that our future is as exciting as our past.

If we take an honest look at Starbucks today, then we know that we are emerging from a period in which we invested in infrastructure ahead of the growth curve. Although necessary, it led to bureaucracy. We will now shift our emphasis back onto customer-facing initiatives, better aligning our back-end costs with our business model. We are fortunate, though, that the challenge we face is one of our own making. Because of this, we know what needs to be done to ensure our long-term future success around the world.

Transforming the *Starbucks Experience*

The Board decided that I should lead this transformation. Given this, effective immediately, in addition to my existing role as chairman, I have returned as chief executive officer for the long-term. Jim Donald is leaving the Company. I want to pay tribute to Jim's leadership. He was a passionate and tireless advocate for Starbucks, and his contribution to our company cannot be overstated.

Looking ahead, the reality we face is both challenging and exciting. It's challenging because there are no overnight fixes. Rather, our success will come in the rigorous execution of several new strategic initiatives ? that capitalize on our heritage to drive our successful future. And our reality is exciting because there is so much opportunity ahead for Starbucks."

Source: **Howard Schultz Transformation Agenda Communication #1**

Schultz letter removed any speculation and rumors about Starbucks transformation, but more importantly, he ensured that his communication was formal to all employees. When you don't communicate during a change especially in the early stages of the change, people will start making up their information. They challenge the goals you have set for the change and criticize the change process, and they imagine the worst that can happen and start to believe their unrealistic assumptions. Rumors run rampant, and they spread like wildfire.

When you are leading a change, you must communicate early, often and right through to the end of the change initiative but you must limit the informal channels of communication. The extent of grapevine communication at Thomas and Co. was alarming, especially during their change process.

This was extremely unfortunate as well as worrying because grapevine communication cannot be substantiated in any real way. From the investigations, many interviewees kept repeating that the grapevine was their primary source of information during the change. The information from the general staff meetings was extraordinarily inadequate, and with the absence of any information from the departmental meetings, the grapevine filled the void. No meaningful communication took place after the general staff meeting.

People will always resist change when the information is inconsistent and this was the situation at Thomas and Co. Information from the general staff meetings was contradictory to what was taking place at the company, as a matter of fact, employees learned about any new change development via the grapevine, as opposed to the formal channels from management, believe it or not.

It is very alarming that any company will value grapevine communication, as opposed to formal communication. If you are communicating to your staff using informal communication channels especially during a change, you should stop immediately. Using this mode of communication to disseminate information to your staff, as opposed to a structured approach to communicating is detrimental to your change efforts.

Van Vuuren and Elving (2008), argued that organizations should try and limit the amount of informal communication as much as possible since this can destroy or disturb all kind of formal communication. But in the absence of formal communication and information according to Fram and Brown (2005), rumors and grapevine discussions are filling the gap.

Galpin (1995), indicated that many change efforts are poorly managed; simply because managers are of the opinion that withholding information ensures that people will learn what is happening only through official channels. But this has proven to be incredibly wrong, and as a result, the grapevine has always bloomed when this happens according to Galpin. Therefore, formal communication activities were often supplemented, and in some cases, usurped by the grapevine according to (Glover, 2001).

However Sinetar (1988), argued a totally different point of view. Sinetar indicated that inflicting an aggressive, formal communication programme upon an organization in an attempt to manage change will not succeed, yet this is what many companies ask their HR department to do. However, an informal communication forum, on the other hand, can encourage brainstorming, active listening, and participative involvement, which can be a powerful tool for managing people and issues during a change process.

Informal communication is 'concerned with the flow of information outside the authorized channels in the organization' (Gallagher et al., 1997, p.584). The importance of informal communication needs to be considered because it will influence the effect of formal communication activities (Brehm, 2002; Glover, 2001; Lewis, 1999; Smeltzer, 1991).

Informal communication fills the information vacuum when formal communication fails to reduce the uncertainty and anxiety that typically accompanies organizational change as alluded by Brimm and Murdock

(1998). The value of adhoc and informal communication should not diminish and replace formal communication for consistency and timeliness.

Every organization according to Dave Berube, has both an informal and formal organizational structure, as well as formal and informal communications. Creating a communication plan within your change management strategy is critical. As mentioned above, you should identify target audiences, determine key messages, choose the preferred sender, and select the appropriate communication channels for that message.

However, when you neglect to develop your communication plan; the desire for information is high, and if the facts are nonexistent, this encourages rumor mongering. Regaining control of information in the midst of rumors is extremely difficult. The longer a rumor is allowed, the more tedious it is to replace with valid information. Many people try to fight rumor with rumor; however, the only effective way to combat rumors is with facts. When many rumors exist, more facts must be communicated to combat the rumors.

Berger and Calabrese (1975), Uncertainty Reduction Theory, suggests that a person experiencing uncertainty will seek information to reduce this uncertainty regardless of the source of information, formal or informal. Although Berger and Calabrese (1975), advocates that management should seek to eliminate informal communication at all levels throughout the organization, they also suggested that management should try to address the issues raised as a result of this informal communication. Management often neglected employees and as a result, that informal channel of communication (grapevine), spreads throughout all levels of the organization like a plague. 99% of the conversation via the grapevine was utterly wrong at Thomas and Co., but with the absence of communication from management, employees felt that this information was gospel, but they were all rumors.

Change, especially a transformational change, a merger or an acquisition, engenders fear in the hearts of many people. If the information is limited, it adds to the anxiety, worse yet, if you hear rumors of layoff and relocation. In cases like these, management should do everything in their power to eliminate this type of rumors with credible information that will allow employees to manage their fears and anxieties.

It is imperative.

Leaders choose to forget that change impacts people, and it is up to the leadership to provide some reassurance to their team with facts, not 'hearsay" or "what was heard by the side." It cannot work like that. Holly Green indicated in her article that employees who spend time trying to find out what's going on, generally don't gain the best or most accurate information.

Rapid, accurate communication is especially important to younger employees who grew up with information at their fingertips. Accustomed to the instantaneous communication of the internet, they feel left out when managers fail to answer their questions, or get them up to speed on projects, changes, or organizational issues. Implementing major change is complex and challenging. Change impacts people, and to successfully lead individuals during a change, leaders must be able to communicate effectively. Holly further indicated that poor communication is the best grapevine fertilizer.

When you communicate with people consistently and frequently, they won't depend on the grapevine. But if you leave your team in the dark on valuable information, and individuals believe they can obtain fairly reliable facts from sources other than the formal channels of communication; your grapevine will inevitably grow and that will derail your whole change process.

I am totally against using and even promoting the use of grapevine communication during any change; it often leads to a heightened level of resistance among employees. However, if the CEO or a manager uses informal conversation with their employees to reinforce what was communicated formally, it is not a problem. These interactions should be encouraged because it allows the leadership to consistently communicate the message of the change.

It is important to note, the information must be consistent with the formal communication from management. If the information has no element of consistency, all aspect of the change will be broken down. It makes absolutely no sense to emphasize consistency if the information is not valid and cannot be substantiated.

6 USING COMMUNICATION TO ERADICATE RESISTANCE

At the 1997 Macworld Expo, Steve Jobs announced that Apple would be entering into a partnership with Microsoft. Included in this, was a five-year commitment from Microsoft to release Microsoft Office for Macintosh, as well as a $150 million investment in Apple. As part of the deal, Apple and Microsoft agreed to settle a long-standing dispute over whether Microsoft's Windows operating system infringed on any of Apple's patents.

Microsoft chairman Bill Gates appeared at the expo on-screen, further explaining Microsoft's plans for the software they were developing for Mac, and stating that he was very excited to be helping Apple return to success. Following Gates, Steve Jobs said to the audience at the expo:

"If we want to move forward and see Apple healthy and prospering again, we have to let go of a few things here. We have to let go of this notion that for Apple to win, Microsoft has to lose. We have to embrace a notion that for Apple to win, Apple has to do a really good job. And if others are going to help us that's great, because we need all the help we can get, and if we screw up and we don't do a good job, it's not somebody else's fault, it's our fault. So I think that is a very important perspective. If we want Microsoft Office on the Mac, we better treat the company that puts it out with a little bit of gratitude; we like their software.

So, the era of setting this up as a competition between Apple and Microsoft is over as far as I'm concerned. This is about getting Apple healthy, this is about Apple being able to make incredibly great contributions to the industry, and to get healthy and prosper again."

Steve Jobs explained at length to the crowd of people at the expo, and by extension to the world why this deal was necessary for Apple. That change prompted the die-hard Apple fans to resist any Microsoft investment at first, but Jobs' ability to emotionally connect with Apple's support was the catalyst that allowed Apple to become the most valuable company in the world today. Jobs used his strength as an excellent communicator to mitigate the resistance.

Resistance is inevitable, change always bring some element of fear for many people, the leadership job is to allay those fears and communicate the benefits of change, especially in the initial stages of the change. According to Dr. Cheng, organizational change often triggers intense emotions, which in some cases can lead to resistance. For example, loss or anticipated loss of control, routines, traditions, status, and relationships can lead to fear, frustration, anxiety, resentment, grief and depression.

Some have compared these emotions to the grieving process associated with major traumatic events such as death and dying. Eriksson argues that in environments of rapid and continuous change, these emotions can be exacerbated by an emotional residue of fatigue and lethargy left over from past change initiatives.

Once the reality of the change starts to manifest itself, a lot of people tend to react negatively, and as such, developing strategies to mitigate resistance is vital. The Change Curve model as illustrated above, describes the four stages most people go through as they adjust to change. It is imperative that leaders recognize these stages, since it will have a significant impact on the outcome of the change, which can be used to determine where the resistance is located, and what strategies can be employed to combat these resistors.

For example, an initial reaction to change may be shock or denial, as employees react to the challenge of the status quo. Individuals who have not previously experienced major change can be particularly affected by this first stage. It is common for people to convince themselves that the change isn't actually going to happen, or if it does, it won't affect them. At this stage, communication is key. Reiterating what the actual change is, the effects it may have, and providing as much reassurance as possible, will all help to support individuals experiencing these feelings.

Stage one is critical, and communication must be a priority. For many organizations this is the "danger zone," and if poorly managed, the organization may descend into crisis or chaos. Again, communication and support will play a vital role to minimize and mitigate the problems that people will experience, for example

- Explaining the why of the change
- The selection of your communication channels

- Tailoring of your message to the different stakeholder groups
- Maintaining consistency in your message, and continuously repeating the message
- Leadership commitment and the important role of the line manager

Making sense,? you see how everything comes together. Good change communications reduces anxiety by explaining what is not changing, and how the organization will act to minimize the perceived downsides of the change. And to inspire genuine belief and confidence, change communications must withstand harsh scrutiny right from the start.

From my analysis thus far, the lack of communication from the general staff meeting at Thomas and Co. left many employees quite confused, as it relates to the changes which resulted in resistance among staff in the organization. Resistance in many instances is inevitable during a change, and it was interesting to learn from the interviewees, how management dealt with resistance.

Question To Employees

Can you please share your opinion as it relates to the strategies used to mitigate resistance to the changes? Was communication used as a tool to eradicate resistances?

Interviewee's Responses

- "Communication was never used as a tool to mitigate resistance."

- "Management simply bypassed staff who disagreed with the changes, and favored those who agreed with the changes."

- "Management developed an approach of bullying the employees to accept the changes."

- "The vision of the change was never used to mitigate resistance."

Communication was not used in any form or fashion to win employees, and sell the change as something viable for the organization. Resistance should also be expected, according to Kotter (1995), but management approach to this resistance will ultimately decide employee's willingness to accept the change. Change is sometimes necessary and inevitable; unfortunately though, employees sometimes view change as a direct attack on their performance, or an unnecessary whim of management.

Change resistance is neither capricious nor mysterious, but in most cases, resistance arises from threats to traditional norms and ways of doing things. As a result, it is a fundamental tenet of human behavior to resist any change.

Michael Armstrong (2007), argued that communication about a proposed change should be carefully prepared and worded, so that unnecessary fears are allayed. It is interesting to note that Armstrong suggested that all available channels, for example, written documents, newsletters, and the intranet should be used. However, face-to-face communication, direct from managers to individuals, or through a team briefing system is always best.

A critical success factor to mitigate resistance is the communication of the vision. Fairhurst (1993), indicated that vision serves to inspire action, focus attention, and create a new social structure in the organization. Moreover, Fairhurst further articulated that a vision that is understood, is more likely to engender a favorable reaction to the change.

John P. Kotter's 8 step change model, also indicated that a strong vision would help determine the success of a change. According to Kotter, it is vital to communicate the vision frequently and powerfully, so it can act as a deterrent to resistance, but it is important to note, that this communication needs to be consistent, frequent, and not a one-off meeting.

The late Dr. Myles Munroe, famous pastor and inspirational speaker, indicated that "vision is the capacity to see further than your eyes can look." If management neglects or chooses to ignore communicating the vision to staff, chances are, the entire process will continue to experience problems, but more importantly, the company will forever be in a change mode with no clear sight of ever changing.

Management must recognize, that vision is that vital tool that inspires people to believe in the change, and as a result, management must first envision what the change will be, and communicate that vision to their staff. It is the responsibility of management to give individuals, especially in the initial stages, the ability to see beyond their eyes in an attempt to mitigate resistance, but more importantly, to win the hearts and minds of staff, and generate that positive excitement about the change.

As mentioned above, never believe that your staff has heard the communication too many times. You have to endlessly repeat the message until it becomes a deeply seated aspect of your employee's daily habit. Be constant and consistent with your message and the vision of the change.

From the interviews, the vision of change lacked in some responses. As a matter fact, when the researcher interviewed the acting HR manager, the HR department did not use the vision of the change as a tool for mitigating resistance. As a matter of fact, none of the managers used the vision in any of their communication with their staff.

The acting H.R. Manager was asked the following question:

Can you please share your opinion as it relates to strategies used by management to mitigate resistance?

H.R. Manager Response

The manager replied that "there was no formal strategy in place; the procedure at that time was to inform the manager if one has concerns, and the manger will highlight the concerns to the HR manager."

No one was aware of the vision of the change. Even though communicating the vision is more likely to engender a favorable reaction to the change; which can be used as a vital resource to encourage dialogue, and sell the change to employees. It was quite surprising that all interviewees were unaware of the vision of the change, and by extension the vision of the organization.

To avoid resistance, change leaders should formulate a more structured approach to dialogue, one which involves the employees. Some of these are face to face communication, questionnaires, formal surveys, and focus groups, as methods for coping with potential and actual resistance to change. Klein (1996), agrees and states that communication can be used to reduce resistance, minimize uncertainty, and improve commitment to change process, this may in turn, improve motivation and retention among employees.

Case Study 2 - Office Relocation at Coastal Petroleum

Coastal Petroleum is a relatively small, but a rapidly growing regional distributor of gasoline, lubricating oils and other petroleum products, that also has a number of gasoline stations in the local market. Its expertise in negotiating contracts with bulk-station operators, and independently-owned chains of gasoline stations, contributes to its success.

The company attracts many of its employees away from competitors, and employees regard a job with Coastal as very prestigious. To date, employee turnover at all levels has been low. Senior management is beginning to worry, however. Over the years, revenues have grown rapidly, profits have not increased in equal proportion and costs have risen significantly. The senior leaders recently set a goal of containing costs, and soon after, an opportunity presented itself to do just that.

The current headquarters of Coastal is in a luxury office building in the centre of the regional capital city near shops, hotels, restaurants and theatres. The rent is expensive, but renewal of the lease, which is about to expire, would mean a substantial increase in the rent. In addition to leasing costs, the office pays high monthly sums for several direct telephone lines to the company's refinery, and bulk-storage terminal.

So, to save costs, management has decided to relocate about 80 percent of its offices to the refinery and bulk storage complex, where Coastal owns the land and buildings. This complex is located in a general area of docks and shipyards, warehouses, factories, and other oil terminals, which are all rather closely grouped together along the waterfront. A large frame building at the plant once housed the company headquarters, but it has sat vacant since the offices relocated to the city centre.

Now the company is planning to move many departments back to this building. To prepare for the move, the building was painted, soundproofed and renovated, to bring it up to modern standards. Although the move is several months away, considerable unrest has developed among office employees. The usual banter and kidding has disappeared, performance has deteriorated, and the group is unenthusiastic about the move, to say the least. Senior management is now worried because they've heard some wildly exaggerated rumors about various aspects of the move.

Employees are complaining about the time they will waste driving to work, about the noise and the dirt of the new location, and the inconvenience of having to remain around the plant during the lunch period to eat at nearby lunch counters. They are used to eating at the better restaurants uptown, where they do not mingle with factory laborers, truck drivers, and other industrial workers. Some are talking about the company 'going to the dogs' and losing its competitive spirit.

Others are grumbling about the 'penny-pinching' attitude of the company, and one of the best salesmen was overheard commenting, "The company is on the down-grade; we are no longer pushing ahead; it's all retrenchment." What should management do? Some have suggested giving employees a raise to compensate for the move.

Others believe that the employees' anxieties will disappear after the move, and are advocating taking a 'wait and see' approach. Still others are in favor of trying to anticipate employees' real concerns and taking action to respond to them. For example, by opening and closing a half-hour earlier than the main shift at the shipyards, employees could have at least an hour to shop and do errands in the city before the stores close.

Source: Communicating During an Organizational Change

Questions

1. What communication strategies would you employ at the company?
2. Can you indicate where management went wrong?
3. How would you use communication to mitigate the resistance at the company?
4. What advice can you provide to management about any future changes at the company?

7 COMMUNICATING WITH INFLUENCE

Why do you buy a product or paid for a service? What motivates your customers to say yes, what motivates your employees to say yes? Have you ever thought about it, really? The list in your mind is probably endless I suppose, but do you think it has anything to do with persuasion and influence.

For a number of years' many companies' have persuaded us the public to buy their products or to try their service using some very catchy ads like:

- Proctor and Gamble Thank you, Mom campaign

- The ever-so-catchy "Every Kiss Begins with Kay"

- Digicel, The bigger better network.

A lot of companies understand the science behind what makes you say yes, and you can thank Dr. Robert Cialdini for it. If you don't know who Dr. Robert Cialdini is, well welcome to the club. Up to a month ago I had no clue who this guy was, I never heard of him before but what got me intrigued is a social experiment video I saw on Facebook named, 'most people are sheep' You guys need to watch that video, very interesting.

It shows an experiment of a person who is only standing when a group of people is standing. The interesting thing is when the person enters the room and notice that everyone in the room is standing, when a horn is blown the person resisted at first. However, after three times, the person who is sitting begins to stand when the horn is blown as well for no reason at all. This experiment led me to Dr. Robert Cialdini book Influence: The Psychology of Persuasion. Cialdini defined this as social proof, people doing what they observe other people doing.

It's a principle that's based on the idea of safety in numbers. For example, when I am feeling for a good doubles; Trinidadians and Tobagonians can attest to this. I will automatically gravitate to the doubles man who has a lot of people around him. I will be very cautious of someone selling doubles who have a few people buying.

But that is the science of social proof. If a group of people is looking to the back of the elevator, the individual who enters the elevator will copy it and do the same, even if it looks funny and that was a proven elevator experiment. Companies use this all the time. Anyone shopping on Amazon can read tons of customer feedback on any product. Some businesses show their Facebook likes and Twitter followers.

According to Jeff Sexton, whether we admit it or not, most of us are impressed when someone has a ton of subscribers, Twitter followers, YouTube views, multiple blog reviews for their upcoming book, etc.

The 6 Principles of Persuasion

Let's look briefly at the 6 principles of persuasion.

Reciprocity

According to 'Influence of Work,' people are obliged to give back to others the form of a behavior, gift, or service that they have received first. So the key to using the 'Principle of Reciprocity' is to be the first to give, and to ensure that what you give is personalized and unexpected.

Scarcity

Simply put, people want more of those things they can have less of. So when it comes to effectively persuading others using the Scarcity Principle, the science is clear. It's not enough simply to tell people about the benefits they'll gain if they choose your products and services. You'll also need to point out what is unique about your proposition, and what they stand to lose if they fail to consider your proposal.

Authority

This is the idea that people follow the lead of credible, knowledgeable experts. Physiotherapists, for example, are able to persuade more of their patients to comply with recommended exercise programs, if they display their medical diplomas on the walls of their consulting rooms. People are more likely to give change for a parking meter to a complete stranger if that requester wears a uniform, rather than casual clothes.

Commitment and Consistency

People like to be consistent with the things they have previously said or done. Consistency is activated by looking for, and asking for, small initial commitments that can be made.

Liking

People prefer to say yes to those that they like. So to harness this powerful principle of liking, be sure to look for areas of similarity that you share with others, and genuine compliments you can give before you get down to business.

Social Proof

When people are uncertain, they will look to the actions and behaviors of others to determine their own. The science is telling us that rather than relying on our own ability to persuade others, we can point to what many others are already doing, especially many *similar* others.

Communication brings influence to life, and communication will determine if your employees and customers respond to your persuasion positively or negatively. I want to share with you two examples to show why written and oral communication must be specifically crafted, to make your influence more impactful.

The Power of Social Proof

Steven Pinker from Harvard University and Dr. Cialdidni, were giving a presentation on the science of communication and the science of style and persuasion at the BX2015, International Behavioural Insights Conference in London. The Park Plaza Hotel hosted the conference, and the hotel was trying to get their guests to reuse their towels and linen for the sake of the environment.

Now using a hotel experiments, Dr. Cialdini showed that the communication on the cards left in the hotel rooms at the Park Plaza was wrong, and it did not generate the level of impact expected. The wording on the cards read something like this:

The Park Plaza

We are on a quest to a sustainable future and we like you to join us in this regard.

According to Dr. Cialdini, the findings from a previous experiment showed the mistake; the Park Plaza should have written on the cards:

The Park Plaza

We are on a quest to a sustainable future and we like you to join your fellow guest in this regard

By that simple change of wording, The Park Plaza would have gotten a 29% increase in compliance from their guests to reuse their towels and linens. To illustrate his point further, Dr. Cialdini stated if the card was crafted like this:

The Park Plaza

We are on a quest to a sustainable future and we like you to join the other people who have stayed in this room in the past just like you in this regard

The hotel would have gotten a 41% compliance from their guests to reuse their towels and linens.

This example is anchored in the principle of social proof where people will naturally follow the crowd. Those simple changes in communication will influence the guests at the hotel to reuse their towels. The change in communication tapped into the subconscious mind of the guests at the hotel, to show that other people were reusing their towels and linens.

Look at this HubSpot ad. To gain more subscription to their marketing blog, the company designs their communication anchor in the principle of social proof.

Join 300,000+ fellow marketers! Get HubSpot's latest marketing articles straight to your inbox. Enter your email address below:

Human beings are highly dependent on the people around them for cues on how to think, feel, and act. We know this intuitively, but experiments have also confirmed this intuition. A crowded restaurant will likely attract more people as oppose to a restaurant with no one in it. It's a proven fact that a person will usually follow the crowd, but here is the added twist. The restaurant will attract more people if it is filled with individuals who are familiar with each other.

Anyone leading a company can apply the same principle. A lot of executives make the mistake of trying to change the culture of their business wholesale, and fall victim to quick fixes that causes more damage in the process. Changing an organizational culture is not an overnight thing, it takes time. As the principle implies, it is best to get groups of people in the organization to change their way of work, and teach others how to enact such behaviors.

That's what the principle teaches you. If you are getting resistance, sell your vision to the senior people, and you stand an excellent chance to get buy-in from your other employees. When an employee recognizes that one of their long-standing compatriots share the vision of the manager or CEO, these employees will be far more convinced to accept the changes as opposed to another speech from the boss, especially if there are trust issues in the organization.

That's why change agents are so valuable and useful within each department, and are usually long standing employees with some degree of influence over other staff members. The wording of your communication will bolster your persuasion strategies and make it more impactful. It is critical that you craft your communication and use the principles of influence as the anchor. In this next example, we will look at a presentation from London Business School given by Mr. Dil Sidhu. In this presentation, Mr. Sidhu shows how a small change in communication improves the fortune for a real estate company.

Mr. Sidhu worked with a group of high-end real estate company that felt like their business was underperforming compared to the other real estate businesses in London. So, Mr. Sidhu's team looked at their lettings department and observed the communication of their employees on the phone with their customers. When someone called the real estate company, the person answering the phone said something like this:

"Let me put you through to Sandra in our lettings department."

The team observing the employees, indicated that the person answering and transferring the call to the letting department was not showing the authority of Sandra, with a simple addition to the communication, the company saw a significant change. The person answering the phone now said:

"Let me put you through to Sandra; she has ten years of letting experience in this area."

That simple change increased the company appointment rate by 20%, and signed contracts by 15%. That simple alteration of communication improved Sandra's credibility and showed her authority in letting.

When Mr. Ghosel became the CEO of Nissan, he communicated to his staff what the company stands to lose if the company did not act differently and quickly. Mr. Ghosel used the power of scarcity to influence his staff to buy into the changes. Scarcity is all about what your employees stand to lose, if they fail to adhere to the changes at the company. Communication brings influence to life, and if you can craft your message to incorporate the principles of influence when communicating with your staff, orally or written, you will be very impactful as a leader, and your change process will benefit tremendously.

If you are wondering if these influential strategies are still relevant after almost 30 years, yeah it is. As a matter of fact, these principles is the foundation for many marketing campaigns, and many companies use them to get you to buy their product or service. Most people can't explain why they made a particular decision but after countless experiments and research, Cialdini was able to identify the underlying factors that influence decisions, and how to use them to get more positive responses.

8 IF YOU WANT TO GROW AS A LEADER, YOU MUST GET COMFORTABLE WITH FAILURE

To achieve the highest success, you have to embrace the prospect of failure. Although this chapter is not related to communication, it is essential that leaders remember that there will be impediments along the way, and you will require some form of inspiration to take you to the finish line.

Whether you are a renowned business owner, executive, politician, father, mother, writer, priest or pastor, I assure you no one is without mistakes, and I am 100% sure they have failed countless times before. Like you, they are human, failure is part of the journey you're on, and no matter how much you would like to avoid it, you cannot. Instead, you must learn how to handle it better and to become comfortable with it.

When James Quincey became the CEO of Coca-Cola, he called upon the rank-and-file managers to get beyond the fear of failure that had dogged the company since the "New Coke" fiasco of so many years ago. Quincey said, "If we're not making mistakes we're not trying hard enough."

According to Pauline Estrem, when we take a closer look at the great thinkers throughout history, a willingness to take on failure isn't a new or extraordinary thought at all. From the likes of Augustine, Darwin, and Freud, to the business mavericks and sports legends of today, failure is as powerful a tool as any in reaching great success.

"Failure and defeat are life's greatest teachers [but] sadly, most people, and particularly conservative corporate cultures, don't want to go there," says Ralph Heath, managing partner of Synergy Leadership Group and author of Celebrating Failure: The Power of Taking Risks, Making Mistakes and Thinking Big.

"Instead they choose to play it safe, to fly under the radar, repeating the same safe choices over and over again. They operate under the belief that if they make no waves, they attract no attention; no one will yell at them for failing because they never attempt anything great at which they could fail (or succeed)."

Some people get paralyzed by failure, and they believe if they fail at something, that's it, my life is over. The sweetest victory is the one that's most difficult. The one that requires you to reach down deep inside, to fight with everything you've got, to be willing to leave everything out there on the battlefield—without knowing, until that do-or-die moment.

Early on in Denzel Washington's career for example, he auditioned for a part in a Broadway musical. A perfect role for him, thought, except for the fact that Denzel didn't get the job. But here's the thing about the story. He didn't quit; he didn't fall back. Denzel Washington walked out of there to prepare for the next audition, and the next audition, and the next audition.

He prayed and prayed, but continued to fail, and fail, and fail, but it didn't matter because you know what? There's an old saying according to Denzel Washington, "if you hang around a barbershop long enough, sooner or later you will get a haircut. You will catch a break."

Fail early, fail often, fail forward.

Last year Denzel Washington starred in a play called Fences on Broadway, and he won a Tony Award, but here's the kicker, it was at that Court Theater, the same theater where Denzel failed that first audition thirty years prior. Do you have guts to fail; if you don't fail, you're living your life so cautiously you are not even trying. To achieve your personal best, to reach unparalleled heights, to make the impossible possible, you can't fear failure, you must think big, and you have to push yourself. Many of us avoid the prospect of failure. In fact, we're so focused on not failing that we don't aim for success, settling instead for a life of mediocrity.

If you want to be great and experience the heights of success like the greats in leadership, you must get comfortable with failure.

9 CONCLUSION

Four companies, Ford, Starbucks, Xerox and Apple, from four completely different industries experienced a phenomenal turnaround primarily because, communication was that integral components used by the leaders to drive home their transformational process.

The findings and recommendation from my research, clearly indicated that Thomas and Co. communication efforts was the major hindrance to achieving a successful change. The research proves that communication should never be an afterthought when planning a change; it is extremely important. As a matter of fact, before I undertook this research, communication was not a pertinent issue I would consider when planning or initiating a change.

However, I can now appreciate and understand that communicating a change via a general staff meeting, or using one communication channel alone with no clear communication structure during a transformational change for example, can erode all efforts to successfully initiate an effective change process.

Change engenders fear in the hearts of many people, myself included, and it is the reasonability of the leader and management to allay those fears, lead by example and inspire your employees to believe in the impossible. As the leader, if you are comfortable with the status quo and you believe communication is not a "big deal" please, take my advice don't start or even plan a change. But with the competitive nature of the world today, if you don't change, chances are your business will cease to exist, and if communication is not a priority during any change, your organisation can descend into chaos and confusion.

It's amazing when you think about it. These four companies have thousands of employees and their change were successful, Thomas and Co. has around 200 hundred employees and their change is still ongoing. Communication in a changing environment is one of or the most critical variable one has to consider when initiating a change. When I decided to pursue this topic, I didn't have a full appreciation for communication, and the magnitude of the problem at Thomas and Co. where communication is concern.

I am eternally grateful that I pursued this research, because I believe with all my heart that every organisation can be great place to work, and I believe that everyone can and should enjoy their work. But the leadership must be armed with the knowledge, understanding, fortitude and skills to create an environment their employees will love. Far to often employees are treated as commodities; discarded and treated like an old piece of equipment with no sense of worth.

It is my hope that this research helps as much leaders as possible because it is quite evident that any company, in any industry, in any sector (private or public), irrespective of the size of the company, small, medium or large, as the leader you are required to understand the role communication plays during a change. It will ultimately determine if your change is a success or a failure.

10 RECOMMENDATION

Chapter 1 - Why Communication is So Vital During a Change

- When leading a change always communicate the 'WHY' to your employees

- Remember communication in a changing environment is one of or the most critical variable one has to consider when initiating a change.

- As the leader, give your employees avenues to express their feedback about the change.

Chapter 2 - Communication Channels

- Use multiple channels of communication during a transformational or complex change.

- Use rich forms of communication for complex change.

- Use routine communication channels for routine change.

- Remember overly rich communication during a routine change will confuse your employees and as a direct opposite, too little information during a complex change will create a lack of trust.

- Face to face communication should be your primary method of communicating during a complex change assisted by other forms of communication channels.

- Social media is a critical communication channel that cannot be ignored.

Chapter 3 - Tailoring Your Communication and Maintaining Consistency in Your Message.

- Communicate constantly and consistently. Never believe for one second that your staff have heard your message many times.

- Be consistent with your message.

- Identify and group your stakeholders. Tailor your communication for each group of stakeholders, but you have to be be consistent.

- Again, endlessly repeat your message until it make an imprint in your staff's subconscious minds, new habits will develop over a period of time.

Chapter 4 - Leadership Commitment and A Line Management Role

- Line managers need to hold regular communication with their staff. This will provide a critical platform for generating support amongst employees since it makes them feel part of the solution.

- Leadership needs to lead by example, and create a culture that facilitates effective communication during the change. Once you give the impression that communication is a waste of time, that spells the beginning of the end of the entire change process.

- There must be follow up meetings between employees and their manager. The management should give their staff the opportunity to question and provide feedback about the change.

- The manager must be aware of the details of the change. If the principal change agent in the department is ignorant to the changes, employees will be even more clueless and resist any attempt to change their mode of operation.

- The management team must buy into the change in attempt to sell the change to their staff. As mentioned in the previous chapter, you must be consistent with your message, it is extremely important.

- If the culture of the organization does not support communication, management should initiate some form of culture change to achieve their objectives as it relates to communicating their change process.

- The leadership culture must lead by example and initiate a culture that supports open and transparent communication.

Chapter 5 - Formal or Informal Communication

- Eliminate informal communication in your organization like a virus especially during a change.

- Information about the change must be formal; there is no sense emphasizing on the consistency of the information when staff have to learn about any new development via the grapevine.

- Management must adopt a formal communication strategy to keep staff informed regularly.

- You cannot authenticate grapevine or informal communication, and as a result, in a changing environment, formal channels of communication is strongly recommended.

Management must recognize, that grapevine communication is a significant hindrance to any type of success. If the information has no element of consistency, all aspects of the change will be broken down.

Chapter 6 - Using Communication to Eradicate Resistance

- Use vision to drive the change and reduce resistance.

- Genuinely listen to your employees' feedback. Don't dismiss your employee's feedback as negative if they don't agree with the change. Have a one on one meeting to clarify your position, and in the process help the employees understand the change.

- In the early stages of the change, resistance is inevitable, communication must be used to mitigate these early resistors. Your communication channels will be vital to help alleviate this resistance.

- Resistance in many cases is resistance to uncertainty, be patient and inspire your staff to change. Lead by example.

- Endlessly repeating the message, create an avenue for feedback and reference the change curve will guide you through the changes resistance phases.

- Help your employees see the big picture.

- Eliminate grapevine type communication like a virus in your organization. Resistance occurs when people are not getting the information from formal channels. Don't allow rumors to become a formal channel of communication.

- Listen for "what is not said and say it."

Chapter 7- Communicating with Influence

- When crafting your message use the principles of persuasion as the anchor.

- Remember the Principles of Persuasion:
- Reciprocity
- Commitment and consistency

- Authority
- Social Proof
- Scarcity
- Likability

REFERENCES

Armstrong, M. (2007). *"the process of performance management". A handbook of human resource management practice*. 10th edition Kogan page Limited. UK pp 131

Allen, R.S., Dawson, G.A., Wheatley, K.K., and White, C.S. (2004), 'Diversity Practices: Learning

Brooks, K., Callicoat, J. & Siegerdt, G. (1979) The ICA communication audit and perceived communication effectiveness changes in 16 Audited organizations. *Human Communication Research*, 5 (2), p.130---137

Balogun, J & Hope Hailey, V (2004) *Exploring Strategic Change*, 2nd ed. Prentice Hall/Financial Times

Balogun, J & Hailey, H V (1999) *Exploring Strategic Change: designing the transition: levers and mechanisms*. Pearson Education Limited. England

Brimm H and Murdock A (1998) Delivering the message in challenging times: the relative effectiveness of different forms of communicating change to a dispersed and part-time workforce, Total Quality Management, Vol.9, No.2/3, pp.167-180

Berger, C. R., & Calabrese, R. J. (1975). Some explorations in initial interaction and beyond: Toward a development theory of interpersonal communication. *Human Communication Research, 1*, 99-

112.

Dess, G. et al., 1998. Transformational leadership: lessons from US experience. *Long Lange Planning*, 31 (5), pp.722-31.

Ford, J. D., Ford, L. W., & McNamara, R. 2002. Resistance and the background conversations of change. *Journal of Organizational Change Management,* 15(1): 105–121.
Goshal, S. and Bartlet, C., 1996. Rebuilding behavioural context: a blueprint for corporate renewal. *Sloan Management Review*, 37 (2), pp.23-26.

Gioia, D.A. and Sims, H.P. (1986), "Cognitive-behavior connections: attribution and verbal behavior in leader-subordinate interactions",

Hiatt (2006) How to implement successful change in our personal lives and professional careers: Building Awareness. United States.

Maurer, R. (1997) transforming resistance HR focus vol 74 NO 10

O'Connor, V. (1990), "Building internal communications (two-way) management-employee communications",

Oshal, S. and Bartlett, C., 1995. Changing the role of top management: beyond structure to processes. *Harvard Business Review,* 73(1), pp.79-88.

Price, A.D.F & Chahal, K. (2006). A strategic framework for change management. *Loughborough University-Construction Management and Economics,* 24, 237–251.

Roberts and O'Reilly (1974) measuring organizational communication. Journal of applied psychology.

Responses for Modern Organizations,'Development and Learning in Organizations, 18, 6, 13 – 15.

Schein, E. (1992). Organizational culture and leadership (2nd ed.). San Francisco: Jossey-Bass.

Senge, P., 2006. *The fifth discipline: the art and practice of the learning organization.* 2nd ed. New York: Doubleday.

Stacks, D. and Salwen, M., 2009. *An Integrated approach to communication theory and research.* 2nd ed. Routledege: Oxon.

Online Resources

Frahm J and Brown K., 2007. First steps: linking change communication to change receptivity [e-journal] 20 (3) Available through: Emerald Group Publishing Limited [Accessed 11 July 2011].

Galpin, T., 2005. Pruning the grapevine [e-journal] 49 (4) Available through: ProQuest- ABI/Inform global &UK Newsstand. [Accessed 22 August 2011]

Insead faculty and research working paper, 2008. The proof is in the pudding: an integrated, psychodynamic approach to evaluating a leadership development programme.
Available at:
http://ketsdevries.com/author/papers/PDF/Proof_in_the_Pudding _Evaluating_LD_programs_WP.pdf
[Accessed 16 march 2011]

Kotter, J., 1995. Leading Change: why transformational efforts fail. *Harvard Business Review*, [e-journal] 73 (2), pp.59-67. Available through: Business Source Complete [Accessed 17 February 2011].

Van Vuuren, M. & Elving, W. J. L. (2008). Communication, sensemaking and change as a chord of three strands: practical implications and a research agenda for communicating organizational change", *Corporate Communications*, 13(3), 349-359. Available through: Emerald Group Publishing Limited. [Accessed 8 July 2011].

Cheng, L. (2015). Enablers That Positively Impact Implementation of Organizational Change, [e-journal] 4(1), pp. 8. Available Through: GSTF Journal on Business Review (GBR)
[Assessed 23 February 2018]

Beatty, C. A (2015). Communicating During an Organizational Change, pp. 8-11. Available through: Queen's University IRC. [Assessed 20 February 2018]

APPENDICES

APPENDIX 1

1.1 - Objectives of Investigation

The objectives of the investigation depict the research problem, questions and objectives below.

1.2 - Research Problem

During Thomas and Co. re-engineering, the leadership of the organisation used a general staff meeting to inform staff of the changes taking place at the agency. This is a onetime meeting and subsequent to this, staff is not inform of further changes at the agency and relied on "grapevine" communication for information. Although the CEO informed line management of the importance of continuous communication with their staff, the general staff meeting was the only medium used to apprise employees of the changes occurring at the Thomas and Co.

1.3 - Research Question

The following research questions provide the researcher with that vital link between the research problem and the specific objectives. Saunders et al (2007), indicated that the clarity of your research questions will ultimately influence one's ability to carry out an effective research, and as such, this enables the researcher to generate specific objectives aligned to the current thinking as it relates to communication and change, but more importantly, seeks to identify the issues surrounding the use of a general staff meeting to outline the change initiatives.

1.4 - Research Questions

- Is a general staff meeting adequate to inform staff of the changes taking place at the Thomas and Co?

- Do managers have the responsibility to consistently inform staff of any changes taken place at the Thomas and Co?

- Can communication during a change eradicate resistance?

- Can "grapevine" communication replace the formal channels of communication at Thomas and Co.

- Can organisational culture support consistent communication during a change process?

1.5 - Research Objectives

- To determine if a general meeting is sufficient to communicate changes to staff.

- To determine if line managers have the responsibility to consistently inform their staff of the change.

- To evaluate if consistent communication by management can be used to eradicate resistance during a change process.

- To determine if Thomas and Co. organisational culture supports consistent communication during the change

- To determine if the grapevine type of communication replaced the formal channels of communication at Thomas and Co.

1.6 - Investigation Design

1.7 - Investigation strategy

The quantity of information generated from the review of current thinking as it relates to the topic for this research, added a different dimension to the entire research. The used of a general staff meeting to outline changes to a staff of an organization, is relatively under research; as a result, an exploratory study, reflecting an inductive approach, was employed to determine the phenomena as it relates to communication and change. More specifically, to highlight the significant influence communication has on the outcome of an organization change process.

The nature and scope of the research relates to the use of a general staff meeting to outline the company change initiatives from the point of view of participants. This makes the exploratory study ideally suited for this research. Sanders (2008) explain that the choice of research strategy will be guided by the type of research and the fact that the research is exploratory in nature; using an ethnography research strategy will be best suited and it the process, allow the researcher to gain insight into management use of a general staff meeting to inform staff of Thomas and Co. change reengineering process.

By its nature, the exploratory study is very flexible and adaptable to change according to Sanders (2008), and as a result, the ethnography strategy will ensure that useful data is collected and generated for the research. In addition, the ethnography strategy will also allow the researcher to develop new patterns of thought about what is being observed and gain insight of management use of a general staff meeting to outline the company change processes from the perspectives of those involved directly and indirectly.

The fact that the research is qualitative utilizing in depth interviews to collect primary data, make it ideally suited for the research. Although, the researcher is closely involved this offered numerous advantages for the investigation. Interviews may take an assortment of forms from fully structured to completely unstructured according to Hair et al (2007:196) however, for the purpose of this research, the researcher employed semi-structured in depth interviews with a limited number of key questions.

The use of semi structured interviews, allow both the researcher and the interviewee the flexibility to probe for more details during the interviews, and as such, the semi-structured interviews encouraged two-way discussion which would have been non existence using questionnaires. In addition, the flexibility of the semi structured interviews also allow for creating questions during the interview, since not all the questions were designed and phrased ahead of time.

The review of current thinking, laid the foundation for the interview questions, as a matter of fact, all the question was generated from the review of the current thinking. Additionally, the questions contained open and closed ended questions, to ensure that the researcher gather rich descriptions of the issues surrounding communication and change at Thomas and Co.

The nature of the questioning allowed for follow up questions to be asked with the intention to probe each topic area further; in an attempt to solicit more response from the interviewee and capture more data for the research. In addition, due to the nature of the research and the limited timeframe to gathered data, the research is best suited for a cross sectional investigation.

1.8 - Sampling Plan

Given the nature of the research, but importantly the design of the research, the researcher utilizes a non-probabilistic approach to select the participants. This method, was used to select specific individuals who was in a number of instances, still directly or indirectly involved in the whole the change process. The interviewees selected, have a number of years service with the company and can honestly give a detail response to the researcher questions. The interviews resulted in a 72% response rate.

The first interview set the tone for the other interviews, simply because, the researcher used this as the pilot and as a result, the researcher changed the approach of the subsequent interviews by adjusting the questioning to fully capture the information from the remaining interviewees (appendix 2 contains a list of the questions). All interviews were recorded with the permission of the interviewee and assurance was given to all participants about the strict confidentiality code of the research. The researcher met all the participants face to face to schedule the interviews, in addition to which, an email was sent to all participants detailing the topic and purpose of the research.

It is important to note, that bias can influence the quality and content of the information gathered from the semi structured interviews, given the researcher close interaction with the respondents. However, to ensure the robustness of the research, the researcher ensured that the interviews span the entire company to achieve that triangulation of the data, in attempt to increase the reliability of the data gathered.

1.9 - Coding the Data

Miles and Huberman (1994), indicated that qualitative research generates a very large amount of data and as a result, some form of data reduction will have to be done to make sense of the information captured. The interviews conducted by the researcher, generated significant amount of information and with meticulous analysis, some data reduction was done to give the researcher the opportunity to transcribe the more salient information which will be more pertinent to the research.

By coding the information, the review of current thinking was used to identify key themes in a visual format to make sense of the data (see appendix 4), but more importantly, coding was also categorized based on the research questions, to show how the data interrelate. Although the coding took a lot of time, a number of transcripts were produced to effectively capture the information for analysis.

APPENDIX 2

Interview Questions

What is your current role and title at Thomas and Co.

Can you please explain if a general staff meeting is an adequate forum management can use to inform staff of the company change process?

Can you please explain if any follow-up was done with you to reinforce the changes outline in the general staff meeting? Tell me to what extent did you have one to one communication with your manager during the change?

Was any evaluation done to determine if you understood what was outlined by your manager, as it relates to the company change process?

Did you buy into the changes at Thomas and Co.? Can you please share your opinion as it relates to strategies used by management to mitigate resistance at the company? Was communication used as a tool to eradicate resistances?

But in the absence of formal communication and information rumors and grapevine discussions are filling the gap. What is your experience where this is concern and can you identify the level of this occurrence at the company?

The use of multiple channel of communication can consistently keep staff informed of the ongoing changes. Can you please give your views on this in the context of the change at the company and the use of a general staff meeting to outline changes to staff?

Can you please indicate if the key messages during the change were tailored for different groups of employees? If no, can you please give your opinion on why this was not done.

Can you please explain your method of evaluation to determine if employees understood what changes was taking place? Was any type of evaluation conducted to determine if a general staff meeting was a good medium to use to outline the company change process?

Can you give your opinion on the company communication culture, as a direct reflection of the leadership culture within the organisation?

Can you please share your opinion as it relates to the strategies used to mitigate resistance to the changes? Was communication used as a tool to eradicate resistances?

ABOUT THE AUTHOR

For the past 10 years, I have dedicated my life towards writing and researching on leadership development and change management, because I passionately believe that leading people is one of the most exceptional experiences anyone can achieve in their career; since leaders have the opportunity to make a profound impact on the lives of many people.

I am a Council Member at German Lehrman Group (GLG) and a member of Harvard Business Review Advisory Council, an opt-in research community of business professionals, involved in research studies, online discussion forums and providing feedback and ideas to HBR editors and product developers on new HBR content and products.

I am also the founder of Leadership First a website committed to publishing the very best leadership articles, one of the leading writers on Quora for Leadership Development, published over 100 articles on LinkedIn focus on leadership development and the author of Communication For Change Management, Mastering Communication to Architect Change.

My articles are featured in the Talent Management Excellence Essentials magazine, the HR Strategy and Planning Excellence Essentials magazine, and Insurance Thought leadership, the world's leading think tank on the subject of Insurance and Leadership.

Printed in Great Britain
by Amazon